Duct Tape Crafts: 48 Duct Tape Projects

Step-by-step Instructions for the Best Duct Tape Crafts that you can complete from the comforts of your home!

By

Kay J. & Patricia L.

DIY Craft & Project Enthusiasts

Join DIY craft enthusiasts, Patricia and Kay, as they take you through their favorite duct tape crafts with detailed instruction and illustrations; help you take your projects to the next level.

Table of Content

Getting Started

Introduction 5

Duct Tape Basics 6

Creating A Basic Duct Tape Fabric Strip 7

Creating A Basic Duct Tape Fabric Sheet 7

Home Décor Projects

Project 1 - Re-Purpose a Table (Illustrated) 10

Project 2 - Spice Up Old Chairs 13

Project 3 - Decorate tea light candles (Illustrated) 14

Project 4 - Add life to a Bland Cabinet with Duct Tape .. 16

Project 5 - Jewelry Tray (Illustrated) 18

Project 6 - Woven Placemats (Illustrated) 20

Project 7 – Drink Coasters 24

Project 8 - Creative Handmade Photo Frames (Illustrated) .. 26

Project 9 - Easy to Make Duct Tape Hammock 29

Project 10 - Pinwheel Table Runner 31

Project 11 - Decorative Wooden Spoons (Illustrated) ... 33

Project 12 – Decorative Outdoor Pillows (Illustrated) ... 35

Project 13 - Wine Bottle Vase 39

Project 14 - Duct Tape Accent Wall 41

Project 15 – Decorative Planters (Illustrated) 42

Project 16 - Decorative Lampshade (Illustrated) 45

Kids & Family Fun Projects

Project 17 – Decorative Mouse Pad 48

Project 18 – Duct Tape Flower (illustrated) 49

Project 19 – Supply Organizer (illustrated) 51

Project 20 - Baby Bunting (Illustrated) 53

Project 21 – Making Lunch Bags (Illustrated) 56

Project 22 - Patchwork Wall Art (Illustrated) 59

Project 23 - Flip Flops 62

Project 24 - Jazz Up Your Stationary 64

Project 25 - Monogram Letters 66

Fashion Accessories & Projects

Project 26 - Boy's Wallet 67

Project 27 – Braided Bracelet (Illustrated) 69

Project 28 – Luggage Tag 73

Project 29 - Accessorize With Hair Bows (illustration) 74

Project 30 – Decorative iPhone Case (Illustrated) 77

Project 31 – Rosette Hair Band (Illustrated) 80

Project 32 – Decorative Designer Shoes 83

Project 33 – Decorative Belt (Illustrated) 85

Project 34 – Fashionable Clutch Bag (Illustrated) 87

Project 35 - Star Earrings (Illustrated) 92

Project 36 - Beaded Necklace (Illustrated) 95

Party & Holiday Projects

Project 37 – Party Mask (Illustrated) 98

Project 38 - Holiday Ornament (Illustrated) 101

Project 39 - Holiday Wreath (illustrated) 103

Project 40 – Candy Cane 106

Project 41 - Gift Bags (Illustrated) 107

Project 42 - Tassel Garlands 110

Project 43 - Gift Wrap Bows 112

Project 44 - Christmas Stockings (Illustrated) 114

Project 45 - Inexpensive Holiday Wrapping Paper 116

Project 46 - Decorative Glass Bottles 119

Project 47 - Gift Tags 120

Project 48 - Cupcake Flags (Illustrated) 122

Introduction

The use of duct tape is no longer limited to packing boxes. Duct tape has found a whole new creative niche for budding crafters. It is versatile, durable and also water proof, which makes it an interesting material to explore. Duct tape is available in a range of colors, prints and sizes to keep your entire family busy for hours.

Here are a few tips and tricks to help you before you get started:

- You will invariably use a pair of scissors to snip and trim duct tape pieces. Use a sharp pair to get the perfect cut. Overtime, your scissors may collect duct tape adhesive on the blades. Dab a few drops of nail polish remover on a cotton ball and clean the scissors. They will be as good as new. Get an X-ACTO for the most precise cuts.

- The duct tape adhesive can get really sticky and form a gunky mess. A hair dryer can come in handy if you want to remove duct tape from surfaces like glass, dry wall, and wood. Keep the hair dryer on low heat and direct it on the duct tape piece you want to remove.

- The heat will melt the glue and the duct tape will come of easily. Avoid the hair dryer setting on high heat to prevent surface paint from peeling off along with the duct tape. The hair dryer trick will ensure that the surface is clean and sticky residue free.

- Always use a rubber-cutting mat to avoid scratches on your working surface. The cutting mats also come in handy when you can't locate your ruler. Use a paper knife when you are required to cut exact measurements. It is easier to use than scissors.

- Don't throw away the last few inches of paper backed duct tape at the end of the roll. Use these to create crafts like little balloon tassels. Use the very last bits of the duct tape roll and you can also think of ways to use the leftover cardboard roll as well.

- Some projects require us to draw a design on the duct tape with a fine tip marker and cut. If you tend to miss the cutting line and are usually left with black lines, consider using a dry erase marker that can be rubbed off after the shape cutting

- Don't ignore the transparent roll of duct tape. This can be used to create a pattern of your choice. If you have a piece of craft paper in a beautiful print that you want to use for your duct tape project, simply cover it up with transparent duct tape and you are good to go. The transparent duct tape covered paper will be waterproof and tear proof.

- When buying duct tape in various designs, go for the largest width available. Instead of buying smaller widths of duct tape, the large sized tape can be further cut into different size strips. This will help save you a lot of money.

- Use your fingers to gently remove any air bubbles or wrinkles that may form when sticking the duct tape together. This will ensure that the tape sticks together and does not come off later.

Duct Tape Basics

From creating a brand new hammock to spicing up old glass bottles, duct tape can come in handy for projects beyond imagination. For many projects throughout the book you will need to be able to produce and use what's called as duct tape strip or fabric. This simply means sticking duct tape together to from either a strip or rectangular piece of fabric that does not have an exposed sticky side.

Creating a Basic Duct Tape Fabric Strip

Duct tape strips are very useful throughout the book as they give you a solid piece to work with. When creating these fabric strips, remember to cut double the length of tape for your desired strip size. E.g. for a duct tape fabric strip measuring 6 inches, you will need a piece of tape measuring approximately 12 inches

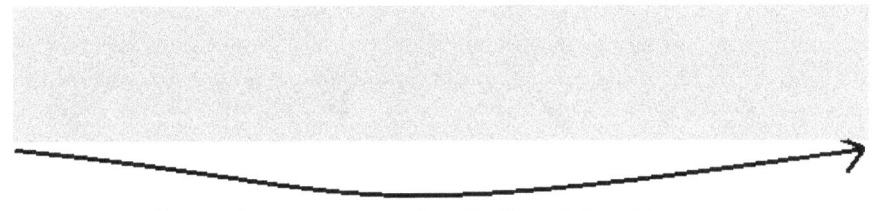

Place the duct tape strip with the sticky side up and fold over into half

Creating a Basic Duct Tape Fabric Sheet

Many times you will need to make a duct tape fabric sheet to complete your project. Here are the four steps in making a solid duct tape fabric.

Step 1:

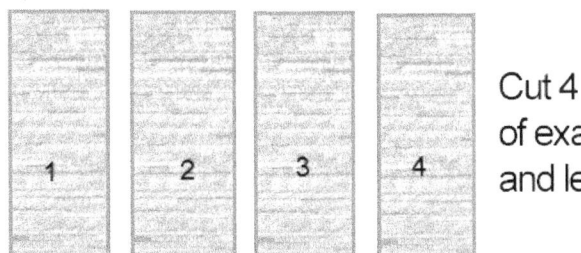

Cut 4 strips of Duct Tape of exactly the same size and leave sticky side up

Step 2:

Now, overlap with 4 more strips laying them horizontally across, again leaving the sticky side up

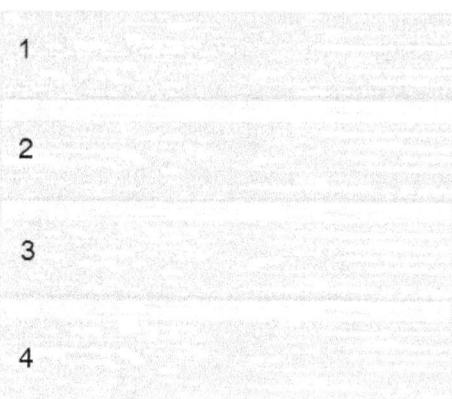

Step 3:

Take 4 more strips and place them vertically, sticky side down

Step 4:

Trim the edges and your fabric sheet is now complete and ready to use

Home Décor Projects

Project 1 – Re-Purpose a Table

Re-using old furniture is a great way to contribute to the environment and release your creative energy. Duct tape can be used to re-purpose an old table, helping add a new style and even give durability to the piece in just a few easy steps.

Materials Needed:

Many different colors and patterns of duct tape

Scissors

Instructions:

1. Clean the original table surface and sand away any bumps or rises in the surface.

2. Think of a design template and draw it on a piece of paper. Some duct tape tables consist of row after row of intermittent colors, while others opt for a checkerboard design with alternating strips of horizontal and vertical duct tape.

3. If possible, take off the tabletop before attaching the duct tape. This will require finding the holes for reattachment, but provides a way for the duct tape to be stretched tighter and installed more securely.

4. Cut the duct tape strips a few inches longer than the face of your table. Adhere the tape strips one by one and tuck the extra bits

under the table for a clean look. Follow your pattern and create the look you desire.

5. Reattach the tabletop if it has been removed and enjoy a good card game on your glamorous new (but not really) table.

1. Clean and sand the surface of the table. Remove legs if possible

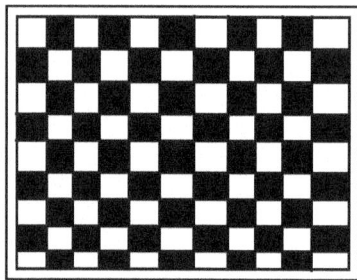

2. Draw a design template on a piece of paper

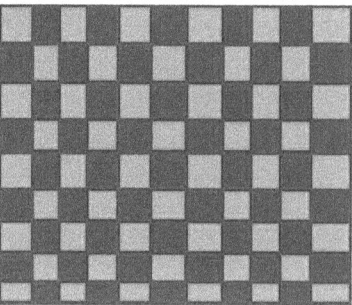

3. Cut duct tape strips according to the pattern and stick them on the table

4. Turn the extra duct tape over the edge and reattach the legs of the table

Project 2 – Spice Up Old Chairs

Comfy chairs are hard to come by. Often times they require years of sitting on to get broken in just right and thus you don't want to get rid of them at the first sign of wear. Luckily some household duct tape can be used to reinvigorate your chair.

Materials Needed:

Duct tape

Scissors

Instructions:

1. If your seat cushion is ripped, the first step to repair is to cut a few strips and cover the rips in both the vertical and horizontal fashion. This will help extend the life of the fabric.

2. Once the rips are covered, you will need to cover the entire cushion or front of the chair for a less tacky look.

3. Measure the length of the chair cushion and cut strips about 2 inches longer on each side. Cover each section of the chair with duct tape strips overlapping each other to keep seams intact and for a clean look. You can even stuff the seat with more cushioning or whichever material is being used before sealing up.

4. Tuck the extra 2 inches of the tape behind the piping to give the chair a more refined look

5. Experiment with placing the tape both horizontally and vertically to create a pattern you enjoy.

Project 3 - Decorate Tea Light Candles

There are never enough tea light holders for the amount of tea light candles in our homes. But instead of spending more money on tea light holders or entirely new candles just because they come with holders, let's decorate our tea light candles with duct tape and make them stand out and more durable.

Materials Needed:

Duct tape in various patterns

Scissors

Measuring tape

Instructions:

1. Measure around your tea light candle to determine the length of duct tape required.

2. Measure the height of the tea light candle.

3. Cut a piece of duct tape according to the measured length.

4. Next, cut the tape into strips according to the height of the candle.

5. Stick it around the candle casing and press down firmly with your fingers.

6. It's as easy as 1 -2 -3. Get your kids to do this for you

1. 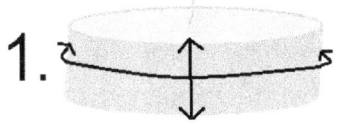 Measure the all around width of the tealight & measure the height too

2. Cut the piece of duc tape accordignly, based on the measured height and length of the candle

3. Cover the tealight with the duct tape

Project 4 – Cabinet Design

The inside of a cabinet is something that is often taken for granted or ignored completely. Decorating the inside of the cabinet is a great way to add some pizazz and to really make it pop with simple designer duct tape. Choose a duct tape design in color or pattern of your choice or mix a few colors to match your home décor.

You will need:

Duct tape

Scissors

Cardboard

Double sided tape

Instructions:

1. Finding the design is the most important part of dressing up the cabinet with duct tape. There needs to be an optimum amount of contrast in order to get the most out of the makeover. (White cabinets can really benefit from a bright background and certain other designs work better with wood. The best thing is that you can change the design whenever you like.)

2. Measure the inside of the cabinet to the exact dimensions. Remember to measure twice before you move onto cutting your cardboard. Even an inch smaller can spoil the look of your cabinet

3. Cut a piece of cardboard according to the measurement. You can join two pieces with duct tape if you need a bigger size. You can

also experiment with making a mosaic pattern by joining several small pieces together

4. Tape one end of the duct tape to a counter and roll it out to the exact length needed. Cut multiple strips and apply it to the cardboard piece. Cover it completely with duct tape. Remove any wrinkles or air bubbles

5. Place the duct tape covered cardboard against the back of the cabinet. Once you are satisfied with the look, use a piece of double sided tape to secure it to the inside wall.

6. To really expose the new design, consider taking the cabinet doors completely off by removing the hinges, thus giving an exposed, open design.

Project 5 – Jewelry Tray

Organizing your jewelry is essential to being able to plan your outfits in style. Very often, at the last minute we realize that one of the earring pairs is missing. For those stressful times, a bright and beautiful jewelry tray is a great asset to own for holding your little jewelry accessories in an organized fashion.

Materials Needed:

Lid of a shoebox

Duct tape in a pattern of your choice

Scissors

Blunt knife

Instructions:

1. Pick a sturdy lid of a shoebox for your tray. You can choose one large lid or several smaller ones depending on how you like to sort your jewelry.

2. Choose a bright pattern of duct tape that matches the décor of your room.

3. Cover the shoebox lid completely with duct tape.

4. Use a blunt knife to press the tape down at the corners to give the tray a neat look.

5. You can mix two patterns or colors or further decorate the tray with glitter.

1. Select desired lid off a Shoebox

↓

2. 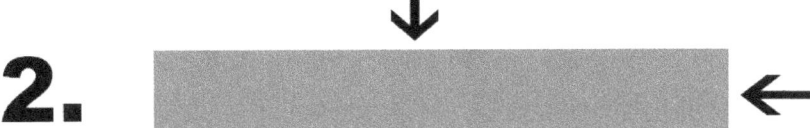 ←

Cover the lid completely with your desired tape / pattern

3. Use a blunt knife to press down on corners to give tray a neat look

Project 6 - Woven Placemats

Duct tape can come in handy if you are looking for an easy, waterproof solution for your dining table placements. Create placemats with duct tape to match your décor.

Materials Needed:

Duct tape

Scissors

Hot glue

Instructions:

1. Since this is a woven placemat, you can choose two or three colors of your choice. Think of the size you require depending on your dining table. The standard placemat size is about 20 inches x 14 inches.

2. Cut duct tape strips of about 21 inches in length. Fold these into half and stick the sticky sides together.

3. Measure the width of your folded strip. If it is about 2 inches then you will need about 7 – 8 of these strips. This is strip A.

4. Cut strips of about 15 inches and again fold them into half. Similarly calculate the number of strips you require. This is strip B.

5. Now, lay one strip B vertically on a table. Dab a dot of hot glue on one end of strip A and stick it onto strip B such that they are perpendicular to each other.

6. Hot glue your entire strip A pieces on to the strip B leaving no gaps.

7. Now interlace all the strip B pieces in an up and down motion to create a woven mat.

8. Cut pieces of duct tape to fold and stick over the edges to secure the strips together.

9. Your placemat is ready!

1. Select and cut a piece of tape to your desired placemat's length. Do the same for your width. (15" and 21" recommended)

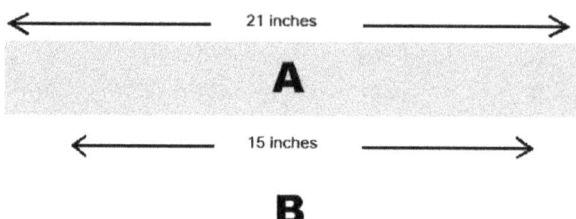

2. Fold each piece from the middle, lengthwise

3. Hot glue strips A on top of strip B

4.

Use B strips to weave into your placemat

5.

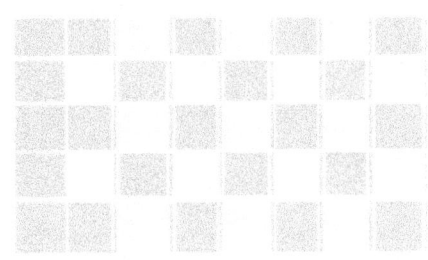

Secure the placemat's edges with duct tape

Project 7 - Drink Coasters

Were you looking forward to entertaining guests, but forgot that you don't have enough coasters to hold all of their glasses? Don't worry. Simple duct tape can help create stylish coasters quickly and at a fraction of the cost.

Materials Needed:

Duct tape

Scissors

Corkboard

Fine point Sharpie marker

A wide mouth bowl

X-ACTO knife

Instructions:

1. Roll out your corkboard and lay it on a flat cutting surface.

2. Place your bowl upside down with the mouth on the cork sheet.

3. Trace the circular mouth of the bowl with a fine tip sharpie.

4. Repeat until you have about 6 circles traced on the cork mat.

5. Use your X-ACTO knife and carefully cut the coasters along the circular marking.

6. Cut two to three strips of duct tape in your favorite print or a print according to the theme of your party.

7. The length of the strip should be slightly longer than the radius of the coaster so that the duct tape can be folded over.

8. Start from the center and press the duct tape onto the cork coaster.

9. Cover the coaster with duct tape strips that slightly overlap each other so that the cork underneath is not visible.

10. Cover all six coaters and you are ready to entertain in style!

Project 8 - Creative Handmade Photo Frames

With digital cameras a lot of us have forgotten the good old photo frames that once decked mantels in homes and desks of offices. This project will give you a reason to print a family photo and frame it in a handmade frame.

Materials Needed:

Cardboard

Duct tape in various prints

Photograph that you want to frame

Scissors

Double sided tape

Ruler

Pencil

X-ACTO knife

Instructions:

1. Use a ruler to draw two squares of 8 inches x 8 inches on a piece of sturdy cardboard.

2. Cut out the cardboard pieces separately so you will have a front piece and back piece.

3. Take one piece of the cardboard square and further draw a rectangle of about 4 inches x 6 inches.

4. Next, use an X-ACTO knife to carefully cut out the 4 inches x 6 inches window from inside the piece of cardboard. Keep it aside.

5. Take your first piece of cardboard and cover it up completely with duct tape.

6. Take your second piece of cardboard with the photo window and cover it with duct tape.

7. Place the two pieces together, joining them on three sides with duct tape.

8. Slip in your photograph from the fourth open side. You can now close this side with duct tape to secure the frame, or leave it open.

9. Now that your frame is ready, stick pieces of double sided tape at the back and hang the frame on your wall

1.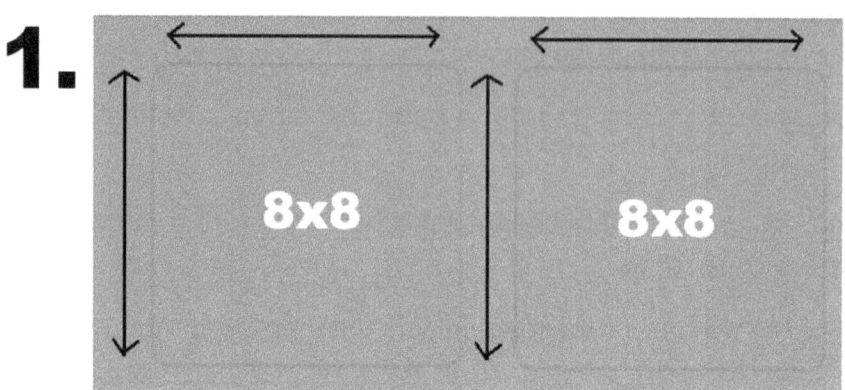

Cut two squares of 8" x 8" from a piece of cardboard

2. Cover one piece with duct tape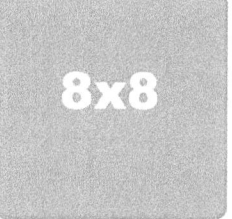

3. 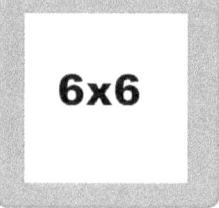 Cut a picture window (6" square) in the 2nd piece and cover with duct tape

4. Layer both pieces together with a picture in the middle. Seal edges with duct tape

Project 9 - Easy to Make Duct Tape Hammock

Hammocks come in handy when you want to spend a leisurely afternoon basking in the glorious sun. You can create a sturdy and waterproof hammock out of duct tape. The thrill of creating a hammock you made will probably be overshadowed by the pleasure of getting to relax on it.

Materials Needed:

3 Rolls of duct tape

2 dowels 4' X 1"

String

Instructions:

1. Secure the dowels in place in your setup area. Screw them into something or simply tape them in place to make it easier to work with.

2. Tape one end of duct tape to a dowel. Run the tape sticky side up under the opposite dowel. Continue over the top back down to the previous dowel this time with the adhesive down. Tape around the dowel to complete one row.

3. Continue making the loops with the duct tape until the entire width is covered.

4. To set up the weaving, place a broomstick over the top of every other duct tape row.

5. Weave the duct tape the horizontal way now in a similar fashion, with the sticky side up at first then looping around with the adhesive down.

6. Your hammock is ready for you to attach to whichever type of hammock setup you've arranged. Carefully test it before you plop yourself on it.

Project 10 - Pinwheel Table Runner

A table runner is a great way to add color and interest to your table setting, especially if you are having guests over. You can create a pinwheel table runner in a matter of minutes and impress your guests with your creative skills. This is a great project for outdoor table setting as well since the duct tape runner will be waterproof.

Materials Needed:

Duct tape in various colors and prints

Scissors

Stapler or hot glue

Ruler

Instructions:

1. This pinwheel table runner is made by attaching several duct tape pinwheels together. You can choose a variety of prints or colors according to the theme of your party or the décor.

2. Start by making a few large pinwheels. Cut approximately four strips of duct tape, 20-inches in length. Lay them down and overlap them slightly to create a large rectangle.

3. Cut four more strips of duct tape and cover the sticky side of the rectangle to make duct tape fabric that is about 20 inches in length.

4. Now, start folding the duct tape fabric in an accordion fold until all 20 inches of duct tape fabric is used up.

5. Press firmly to create the creases. You can also leave the according fold duct tape fabric under some heavy books for a while.

6. Now snip the ends into small triangles or create your own design. You can leave it alone if your wish.

7. Unfold and stick or staple the two ends together to create a pinwheel. This will be in the shape of a circular disc.

8. Continue making pinwheels of different sizes and then join them together to form a long table runner.

9. Lay it on the table and enjoy the compliments!

Project 11 – Decorative Wooden Spoons

Sometimes your kitchen needs a jolt of brightness to make cooking and baking an interesting chore. You need not go to great lengths to procure colorful decorative pieces for the kitchen; you can quickly add some color by starting with your old wooden spoons.

You will need:

Old wooden spoons

Duct tape in various colors and prints

Scissors

Clear gloss spray

Instructions:

1. Wash and dry your old wooden spoons.

2. Cut small pieces of duct tape using different colors and prints. Then, further cut thinner strips in different sizes.

3. Wrap the strips of duct tape around the wooden spoon starting at the bottom.

4. Make a pattern with different colors and prints and finish halfway to the top.

5. Finally spray your wooden spoon with clear gloss spray and place them with the bottom up in a glass jar.

6. Remember that these spoons are for decoration only and should not be used. If you want to use these spoons then just skip the clear gloss spray.

1. Clean and dry your old wooden spoons

2. Cut duct tape strips of different widths

3. Cover just the handle with your strips in any pattern you desire

Project 12 – Decorative Outdoor Pillows

Outdoor pillows, if left outside in harsh sun or rain can get spoilt no matter how hard wearing they may be. Since duct tape is waterproof, a duct tape pillow can be left outside without worrying about it. It does not get soaked in the rain and will come in handy on road trips. It is cheap and easy to make in a range of colors and prints to suit your outdoor décor.

Materials Needed:

2 rolls of duct tape in colors and prints of your choice

Scissors

Fiber Fill

Newspaper

Instructions:

1. Depending on the size of the pillow you require, trace out a pattern on the newspaper. This will make sizing your pillow easier.

2. Now, cut duct tape lengths according to the size and lay them flat with the sticky side facing up.

3. Adhere the strips together slightly, making a rectangle approximately the size of the traced pattern.

4. Now repeat on the sticky side of the rectangle to make duct tape fabric.

5. Make another piece of the duct tape fabric in the same size following the newspaper pattern. You will now have two sides of the pillow

6. Join the two pieces together with duct tape on three sides leaving one side open.

7. Fill in the pillow with fiber making it plush and cushy. You can also insert a pillow of the same size if you like

8. Close the open side of the pillow with duct tape and you are ready to bask in the glory of your handmade pillow.

1. Trace out the size of your pillow on a newspaper

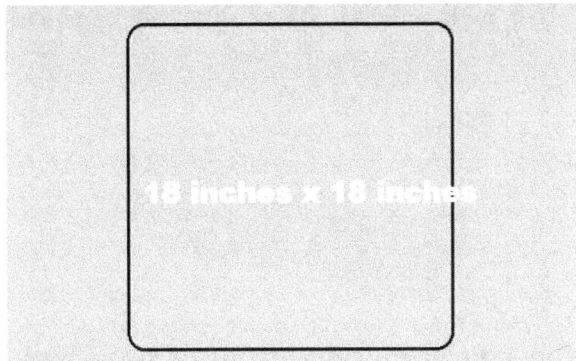

2. Make 2 pieces of duct tabe fabric sheets based on the sizes of your newspaper tracings

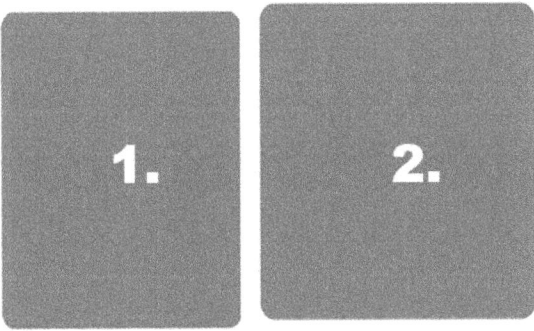

3. Join the 2 pieces together with duct tape on the sides, but leave one side open

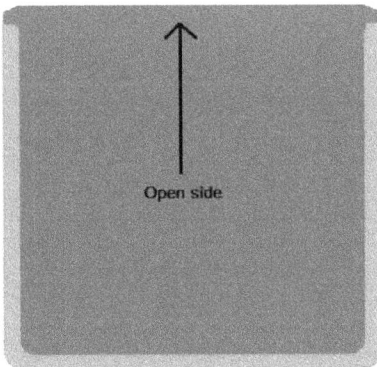

4. Stuff the pillow with fiber via the opened side

5. Seal the last opening with duct tape and enjoy!

Project 13 - Wine Bottle Vase

You can use old wine bottles to craft interesting vases. Wine bottles creatively decorated will add a touch of color to your home décor.

Materials Needed:

Old wine bottles

Spray paint in white or gold

Duct tape in various prints

Scissors

Measuring tape

Spray gloss finish

Instructions:

1. Clean the wine bottles with fresh, running water and dry them completely.

2. Pick a spray paint in a color of your choice and paint the wine bottle. Use at least two coats of paint to cover the bottle completely.

3. Leave the bottle to dry before working on it any further.

4. Once it is dry, measure the circumference of the bottle at different heights.

5. Cut duct tape strips of different colors and prints according to the sizes measured.

6. Cut these into thinner strips and apply them on the bottle creating a design.

7. Use your imagination to decorate the bottle with duct tape.

8. You can also cut various shapes like dots and stars to decorate the bottle.

9. Finally once you are satisfied with the design of your wine bottle vase, finish it with a few coats of clear gloss spray.

10. Fill the bottle with water and add a few stems of beautiful flowers into your new vase.

Project 14 - Duct Tape Accent Wall

You can cover your wall with duct tape stripes to create a wonderful accent piece. If you are tired of living with bare walls, duct tape can help you rev up the décor in your room. You will need help for this project, but this is easier and quicker than a paint job.

You will need:

Duct tape in various colors and prints

Scissors

Painter's measuring tape

Instructions:

1. Draw the pattern you want to create on a piece of paper. This will help you remember the sequence of colors and prints of duct tape you need to use.

2. Measure the length of the wall you intend to cover and start from the top.

3. Carefully adhere your chosen duct tape to one corner and pull it across the width of the wall to create horizontal stripes. Then, pull the duct tape along the length to create vertical stripes. You need help to make sure it is neat and tidy

4. Apply a second duct tape design overtop of this base layer.

6. Your wall is now as good as new. Place a comfortable chair and pillows matching the colors of the stripes underneath to make the wall stand out.

Project 15 – Decorative Planters

Perk up your garden with decorative planters. You do not need to invest in a whole lot of new planters for spring, just use duct tape to bring them back to life. This project will help you hide the wear and tear that the harsh weather might have brought onto your planters.

You will need:

Planters

Duct tape in a range of colors

Spray paint in a color of your choice

Scissors

Spray sealant

Instructions:

1. Remove your plants from the planter if possible. If not then cover it with some newspaper or waste pieces of cloth.

2. Sand away the planter to remove mud and grit.

3. Once the surface is clean, spray paint the planter with a color of your choice. White will make your plants stand out and your garden will appear fresh.

4. Let the paint dray and then re-coat it again.

5. Meanwhile, think of designs you would like to create on your planter. Vertical stripes will make your plants appear taller.

6. Cut strips of duct tape in random lengths and then further cut them into thinner strips.

7. Apply them on the planter vertically overlapping each other in some places to create a design.

8. Cover the entire planter with vertical stripes of different lengths.

9. Once you are done, seal the paint and duct tape design with a spray sealant.

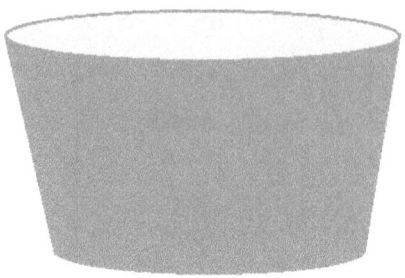

1. Sand and clean your planter

2. Spray paint planter with white color

3. Cut Strips of Duct Tape of varying widths

4. Cover planter in design of your choice

Project 16 – Decorative Lampshade

Are you bored with your existing lampshades, but cannot think of spending through the nose for new ones? Duct tape can help re-purpose your old lampshade into a brand new one. It is easy and you can make a design of your choice.

Materials Needed:

Old lampshade

Duct tape in your choice of colors and patterns

Scissors

Instructions:

1. Cut the fabric off the your old lampshade such that you have only the lampshade frame to begin with.

2. Look for an old lampshade in a thrift shop before cutting off your existing one. You can practice and then work on the real one once you are satisfied.

3. Think of a design you like. Stripes or printed duct tape will help enhance the beauty of your lampshade.

4. Measure the top to bottom length of the shade and cut a strip of duct tape with a little excess to fold over.

5. Stick your duct tape strips on the top and pull them down, securing them at the bottom.

6. Repeat till you have a pretty pattern and the entire shade is covered with duct tape.

7. You can now re-screw your newly revived lampshade on your lamp.

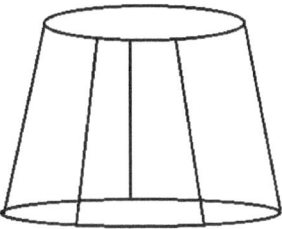

1. Remove fabric from old lampshade, so you have just the frame to work with.

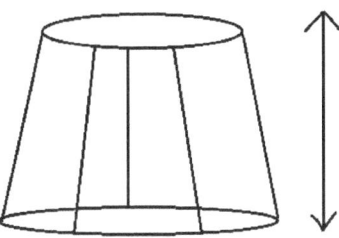

2. Measure the lampshade and cut duct tape to matching lengths in various colors.

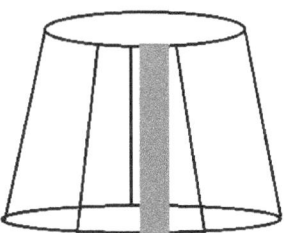

3. Starting from the top, attache strips to the frame according to your choice of design

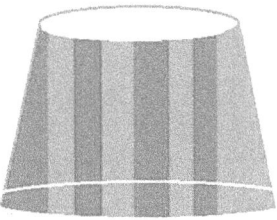

4. Cover entire lampshade with your strips and reattach.

Kids & Family Fun Projects

Project 17 – Decorative Mouse Pad

Add a bit of color to your boring computer table by creating a duct tape mouse pad in exciting prints and colors.

Materials Needed:

Duct tape

Scissors

Cardboard

Ruler

Instructions:

1. Mark a square of approximately 8 inches x 8 inches on a piece of cardboard.

2. Cut the cardboard. This will be the base of your mouse pad.

3. Cut strips of about 9 inches in length and stick them on the cardboard piece. Fold over the extra length onto the back of the cardboard.

4. Make a pattern or keep it solid.

5. Cover the cardboard completely and your mouse pad is good to go!

Project 18 – Duct Tape Flower

Flowers are a welcome sight to any area of the home. Unfortunately, depending on the time of the year flowers can be a seasonal thing. A good way to add some color, style, and thoughts of spring to your home is with a duct-tape flower arrangement.

You will need:

Colored duct tape

Small stick

Scissors

Instructions:

1. Cut approximately a 2-inch strip of duct tape.

2. Fold the right corner of the strip down and adhere it. Then bring the left top cornet down to create a triangle. But make sure to leave some of the sticky adhesive showing

3. Take a small stick and place the adhesive side to the corner. Angle the stick and roll up the duct tape piece to create the appearance of a petal with the duct tape triangle (like a little flag).

4. Repeat the steps, layering each piece over the previous one in the same direction. Continue until you have a beautifully blooming flower. You can experiment with a mix of colors.

5. Wrap green duct tape around the stick to create a stem. Continue making the flowers until you have a bunch to decorate with.

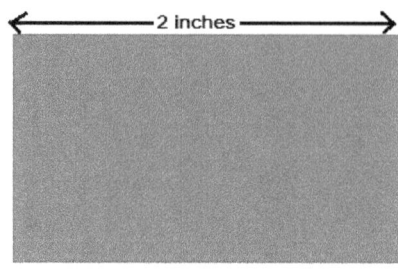

1. Measure and Cut 2 Inch piece of Duct tape

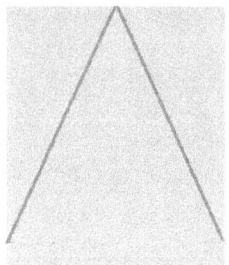

2. Fold the two top corners down to form a triangle

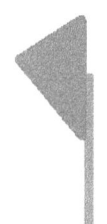

3. Attach remaining strip of tape around the stick to form a pedal

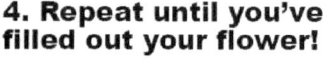

4. Repeat until you've filled out your flower!

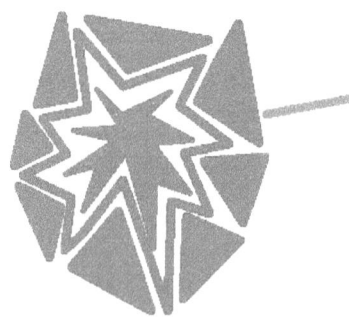

Project 19 - Supply Organizer

A well-organized study table means that you do not need to waste time looking for supplies like writing instruments, staplers and other essentials. Keep your study table organized with a handmade supply organizer. It is quick to make and efficient to use.

You will need:

Empty beef jerky can or similar type can

Duct tape

Scissors

Instructions:

1. Cut two pieces of duct tape and slightly join them together to form a larger rectangle, leaving the adhesive side facing up.

2. Trace the bottom of the jerky can on the duct tape and cut out the round pattern. Adhere it to the bottom of the can.

3. Wrap the outside of the beef jerky can in a decorative duct tape pattern.

4. Add design contrast by putting a contrasting colored duct tape pattern on the top, bottom and through the middle.

5. Join a few duct tape covered cans together to store all your supplies together.

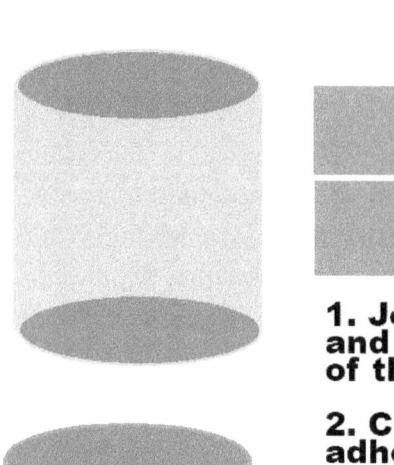
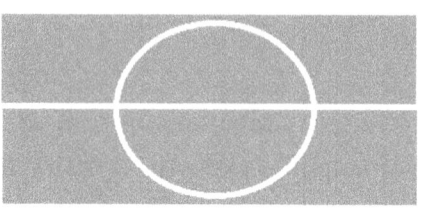

1. Join two strips of tape and trace the bottom of the can.

2. Cut out and adhere to bottom.

3. Wrap the siding of the can with duct tape

4. Contract can with different colors and patterns with tapes

Project 20 – Baby Bunting

A beautiful baby bunting will be a wonderful and welcomed addition to your child's bedroom. These can be customized in various colors for babies, kids and teens. You can also create smaller strings of buntings to wrap gifts or decorate your home.

You will need:

Duct tape in light pink or light blue for a baby's room

Baker's twine or jute twine

Scissors

Instructions:

1. Cut approximately 3 strips of duct tape, 16 inches in length

2. Lay them on a cutting surface with the sticky side up. Slightly join the three strips together to create a rectangle. Place the rectangle vertically on the surface so that when folded into half it is about 8 inches in length (don't do it yet).

3. Cut a long length of the twine and place it in the middle across the rectangle sheet of tape. Leave a little twine on the side for hanging (depends on how much slack you want to leave).

4. Now fold over the top half of the duct tape sheet and adhere the sticky sides together with the twine in the middle. The folded rectangle should sandwich the twine.

5. Shape your bunting by cutting the duct tape rectangles into triangles. Be careful while cutting and do not snip the twine off. Leave a little space between two flags.

7. Decorate with the baby's name or words like peace, joy etc. and the bunting is ready to hang.

16 inch

1. Cut 3 16 inch strips and join together to form a rectangle

2. Run a baker's twine down the middle

3. Fold rectangle over and cut into triangle

4. Repeat on same twine to form baby bunting.

55

Project 21 - Making Lunch Bags

Do you sometimes find yourself without lunch because someone took your lunch bag? The perfect plan of attack is to craft your own duct tape lunch bag so your original design will be easily noticeable and different from the other brown lunch bags.

Materials Needed:

Plastic bag

Duct tape

Scissors

Measuring tape

Instructions:

1. The plastic bag will serve as your insulation. To begin, cut two rectangular pieces approximately 18 inches x 8 inches in size from the plastic bag. You can vary the measurement as per your need. You can also trace out the pattern of your existing lunch bag.

2. Cover one complete side of both the rectangles with duct tape, using any pattern and row design you like.

3. Place the two rectangles together with the plastic side inside and seal it by placing duct tape around the edges.

4. Cut two more duct tape pieces to serve as the handles. Tape each of them to the inside of both sides of the bag.

5. In minutes you have created an insulated lunch bag that cost pennies. Experiment with different colors or sayings such as "KEEP OUT".

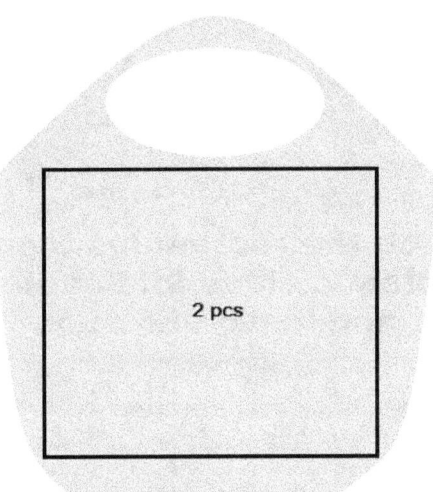

1. Cut two large rectangles from an ordinary plastic bag

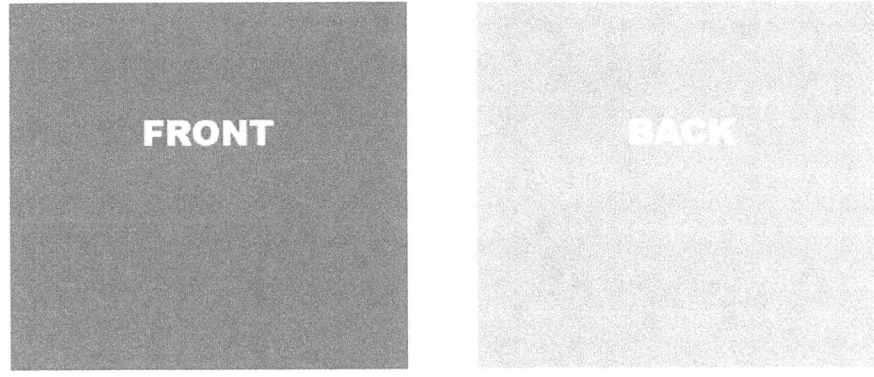

2. Cover the rectangles with duct tape on just one side

3. Place the rectangles together, with the plastic sides in. Seal three sides and leave one open

4. Create handles with duct tape strips and complete the bag

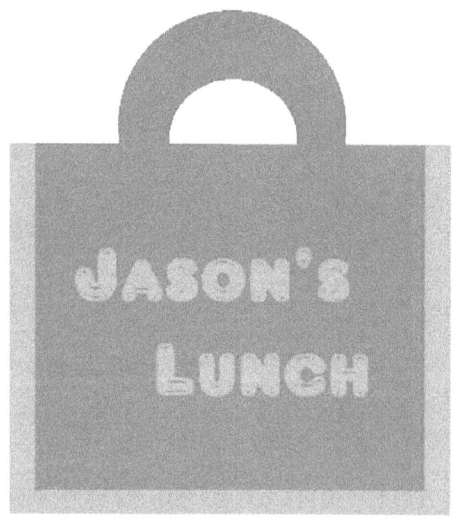

5. Decorate with your own flair

Project 22 - Patchwork Wall Art

With the number of duct tape designs available in the market these days, it is possible to make a few wall art masterpieces to deck up the walls of your home. These bright duct tape wall art pieces in the kids' bedroom will keep the room looking bright and cheerful. It is easy enough for the kids to make their own wall art out of duct tape. Take inspiration from the American patchwork quilts and get started.

Materials Needed:

Duct tape in various colors and prints

Scissors

Poster boards

Command strips

Instructions:

1. Choose a poster board in a size of your choice.

2. Choose the duct tape prints and patterns you would like to use. Take interesting contrasting colors to make your wall art stand out.

3. Start from the middle and lay your first duct tape design diagonally across the poster board.

4. Stick it to the poster board and move onto laying the next piece down.

5. Cover the board with diagonal strips of duct tape.

6. Once the entire board is covered, flip the board over and use a sharp pair of scissors to snip the extra duct tape off.

7. You wall art is ready, create three more poster boards in a similar fashion and create a patchwork wall art.

8. Hang it on the wall!

1. Choose a poster board in a size of your choice

2. Cut duct tape strips in colors and patterns of your choice

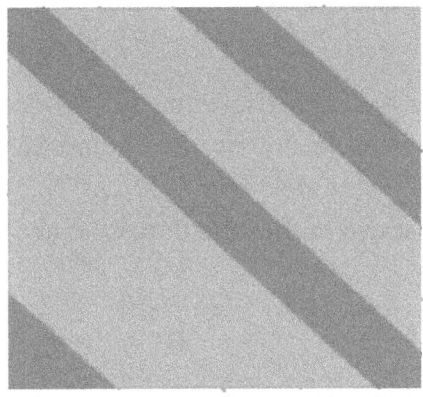

3. Cover the poster board with duct tape places diagonally across.

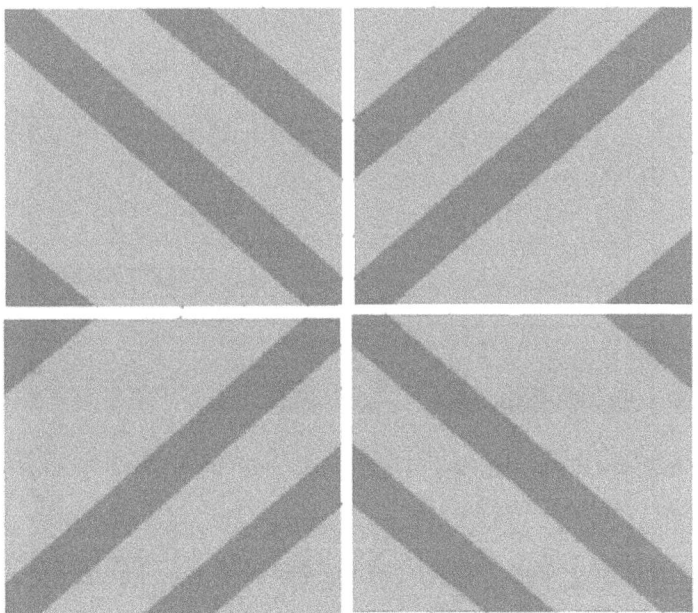

4. Create 3 more poster boards to complete your patchword wall art

Project 23 – Flip Flops

Did your little furry buddy chew up your flip-flops? Don't worry you can quickly craft a replacement pair of flip-flops from duct tape while you wait for your new pair to arrive. This works great as a short-term replacement, but the bottom is not very thick. So watch your step!

Materials Needed:

Cardboard

Duct tape in a color of your choice

Scissors

Fine tip marker

Instructions:

1. Put your feet on the piece of cardboard and trace out an adequate flip-flop design.

2. Cut out each cardboard piece and cover it with the colored duct tape you want for the base.

3. Cut four long pieces of duct tape for the straps and fold each one in half.

4. Poke holes in the cardboard with the end of the scissors, two holes in the back and one between the big toe. You can use a punch or a sharp pair of scissors.

5. Thread a strap from the front to the back on each flip-flop. Try them on and adjust the strap to the desired length, cutting off the excess.

6. Tape the straps to the bottom of the cardboard and place a piece of tape near the toe so the two straps don't separate.

7. Remember to secure the straps with duct tape to the base of the flip-flop.

Project 24 – Jazz Up Your Stationary

Your stationary will stand out from the rest and you will be able to find that missing pen much more easily.

Materials Needed:

Duct tape in various colors

Scissors

Stationary supply like pens, paper clips lanyards, stapler

Instructions:

1. Covering pens with duct tape is very simple. Choose a print that you really like or use two different ones if you like.

2. Simply roll the duct tape around your pen and it is ready with a sharp new look. You can cover pencils as well, but sharpening them with a layer of duct tape will be difficult

1. To jazz up your stapler simply tear a piece of duct tape and trace out the top and the bottom of the stapler.

2. Cut according to the pattern and stick on the two sides

1. You can cover a lanyard to make it look pretty. Cut short strips of duct tape approximately 6 inches in length. Start at one end and lay your lanyard in the middle of the duct tape strip

2. Fold over the two sides to secure the tape firmly on the lanyard. Cover the entire piece with strips of duct tape. You will need broad duct tape to fully cover the lanyard.

You can similarly cover a number of stationary items to create your own designer range. Patterns work extremely well in these situations when you wish to coordinate designs across the variety of office items.

Project 25 - Monogram Letters

Using monogram letters can be a great way to decorate your children's' bedrooms. Instead of buying them, it is easy to use duct tape to fashion cute monogram letters.

Materials Needed:

Cardboard monogram letters from a thrift store

Duct tape in bright colors

Scissors

Instructions:

1. Choose two contrasting colors for your monogram letters.

2. Cut strips of duct tape in one color and cover the face of the cardboard monogram letter.

3. Flip over and use an X-ACTO knife to trim the extra bits of tape.

4. Use the second color of duct tape to cover the sides of the letter.

5. This will give your monogram letters a three dimensional appearance.

6. You can further decorate the letters with a duct tape bow or use it as is.

7. Hang it on the wall or place it anywhere inside the room, like on a dresser!

Fashion Accessories & Projects

Project 26 - Boy's Wallet

Impress your friends with a homemade wallet, one completely made out of duct tape. Besides being cool, it is also waterproof; it will keep your money safe and make a statement at the same time.

Materials Needed:

Duct tape in various colors

Scissors

Ruler

Instructions:

1. Cut about 4 pieces of duct tape approximately 9.5 inches in length.

2. Lay them down on your table with the sticky side up.

3. Take one of these strips of tape and overlap it on the bottom edge of the second strip, similarly continue till all the strips adhere together, forming a rectangle with the sticky side still up.

4. Cut 4 more strips of the same size and cover the sticky side to make a duct tape sheet.

5. Trim the sides to create your rectangular sheet about 9 inches x 6 inches.

6. Cut another piece of tape that is about 9-inches in length. Then cut it into half down the middle. Take those two pieces and fold them over on the top and bottom of the rectangle sheet to smoothen the rough edges.

7. Next, fold your duct tape sheet into half and make a crease at approx. 4 ½ inches from the edge. Keep it aside.

8. Follow steps 1 to 4 to make another duct tape sheet. This will be used for the money pocket.

9. Cut six duct tape sheet rectangles of about 4 inches x 1-½ inches for the credit card pockets.

10. Pull out your wallet base and line up three pockets on the top left hand side and the other three on the top right hand side.

11. Leave about 1 ½ inch space between each pocket when lining them on either side.

12. Cut some duct tape and secure the pockets down the middle and the two sides.

13. Flip over so the pockets are facing down.

14. Attach your second duct tape sheet atop of your wallet.

15. Cut a 6-inch piece of tape into half down the middle and conjoin the two fabric sheets to form the money pocket.

15. Finally trim off any extra pieces of duct tape, fold in half and voila! Your wallet is ready!

Project 27 – Braided Bracelet

With the amount of designer duct tape being produced today, it is easy to make stylish handmade bracelet for your friends and family. Make these for a family picnic or for your group of buddies at school.

You will need:

Two or three colors of duct tape

Measuring tape

Scissors

Instructions:

1. Measure around your wrist and cut three strips of duct tape from different colors, leaving an inch or two more than the measurement.

2. Fold each strip tape in half with the sticky side on the inside, creating fabric strips.

3. You should now have three equal strips of three colors. You can trim it down the side to make the strips thinner if you like.

4. Cut a small piece of duct tape and use it to tape all three strips together at the end

5. Repeatedly twist the left and right strip over the middle piece, making a braided pattern.

6. Tape the end of the braid together to keep the bracelet in place.

7. Test out the bracelet on your wrist. Cut some off if it's too loose otherwise use another piece of duct tape to secure the bracelet around your wrist.

8. You can also experiment with different clasping techniques to make a bracelet that can be removed and reattached.

1, Cut 3 strips of tape according to your wrist size measurements

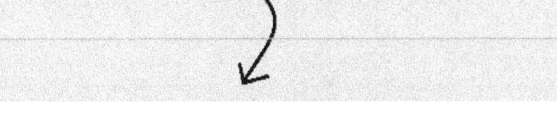

2. Fold each strip in half

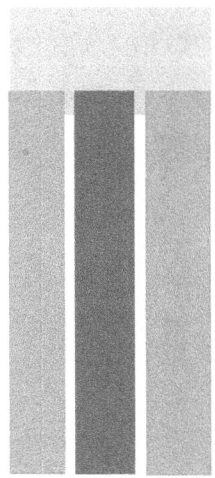

3. Stick the 3 stripc on another piace of tape

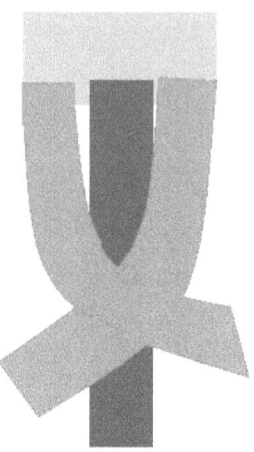

4. Braid the 3 strips by moving left to right over the center strip.

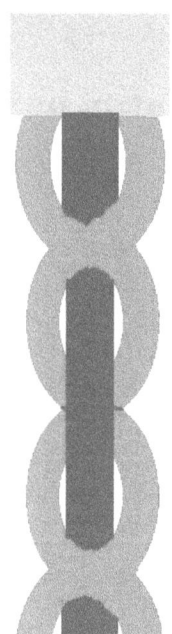

5. Wrap your bracelet around your wrist and secure with a piece of tape or adhere a jewelery clasp

Project 28 - Luggage Tag

Travelling can be stressful and the last thing you need is a lost baggage. Using bright colors of duct tape will help you easily recognize your luggage as it comes out of the baggage carousel.

Materials Needed:

Colored duct tape

Punch

Black marker

Instructions:

1. Cut out three pieces of duct tape according to the length you want the luggage tag.

2. Join the three strips together at the bottom to form a large rectangle. Repeat with the sticky side and create a duct tape fabric sheet.

3. Cut out a unique design or letter of your name out of the duct tape fabric.

4. Punch a hole in the top of the luggage tag.

5. Cut a long piece of duct tape, cut it in half and conjoin, then fold it twice to make string to attach the tag to the luggage.

6. Write your name and address on the luggage tag just in case your suitcase gets lost.

Project 29 - Accessorize with Hair Bows

A duct tape hair bow will keep your hair in place and ideally match your outfit. Make one in a jiffy! Experiment with different colors of designer duct tape to really accentuate your wardrobe.

You will need:

Duct tape in various colors and patterns

Scissors

Bobby pin

Hot glue

Instructions:

1. Cut a piece of duct tape approximately 5 inches long. You can also experiment with a size of your choice to make smaller or larger bows.

2. Fold the duct tape inwards with the sticky sides together, leaving you with a 2-½ inch piece fabric strip. Remove any wrinkles or air bubbles with your fingers.

3. Next, make an accordion by folding this piece three times lengthwise. Press hard to achieve the perfect fold.

4. Cut another small piece of duct tape, only about ½ inch. You can choose a different color or pattern for this to make your bow stand out.

5. Pinch the accordion piece in the middle and wrap the shorter piece around to keep it in place.

6. Hot glue the little bow to your bobby pin.

7. Make several small bows and cluster them together to make a beautiful hairpiece.

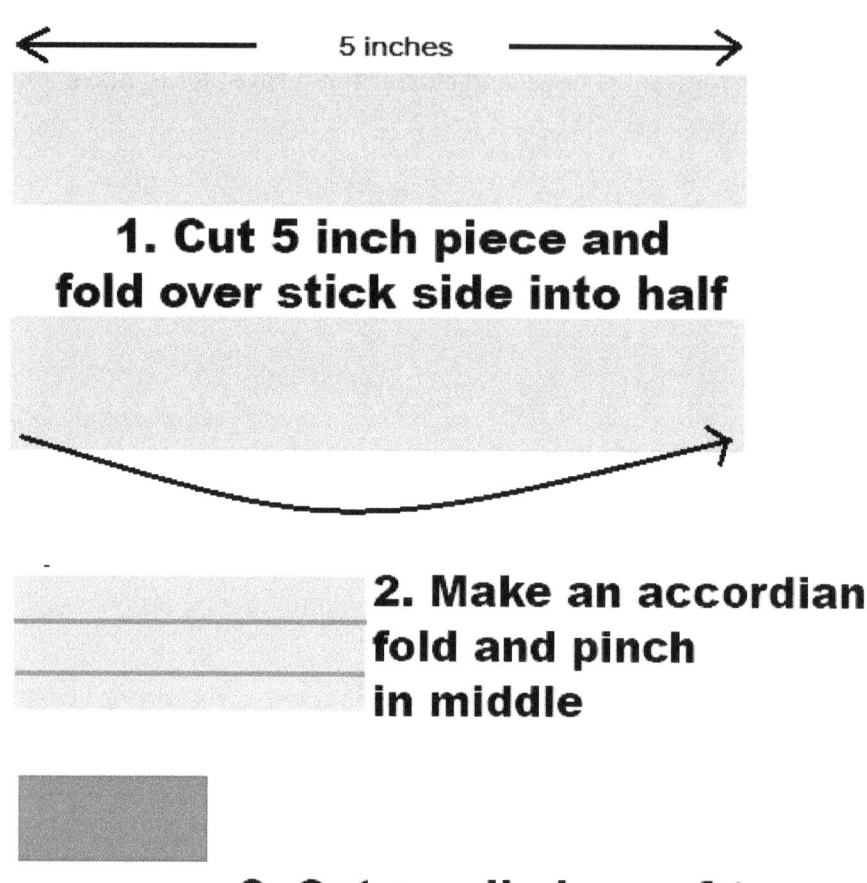

Project 30 – Decorative iPhone Case

If you are looking for an easy way to jazz up your iPhone case, then colorful duct tape can come in handy. Use strips of duct tape to decorate or cut shapes like stars and hearts to add a new life to your old case.

Materials Needed:

An old iPhone case

Duct tape in various colors

Metallic paint

Scissors

Ruler

Clear Gloss finish

Instructions:

1. Clean the back surface of your old iPhone case.

2. Think about a pattern that you would like to create with duct tape. For example, you can horizontally paste strips of tape and add a few lines of silver or gold metallic paint in the middle.

3. Measure the width of the case and cut the duct tapes.

4. You will need to further cut the tape strips into thinner strips to create a stripy pattern. Vary the thickness of each strip.

6. Paint the case in silver or gold metallic paint and let dry.

5. Once fully dry, adhere the strips on the iPhone case leaving 1 or 2 cm gap in the middle

7. Spray a coat of clear gloss finish.

1. Clean the surface of an old iPhone case

2. Cut thin strips of duct tape

3. Cover case with stripy pattern and a few strips of metallic paint. Finish with a coat of clear gloss

Project 31 - Rosette Hair Band

Don't throw away your old hairbands! These can be revived very easily using pretty duct tape prints and patterns. Decorate your hairbands with duct tape flowers and bows, helping you make a fashion statement with your wardrobe.

Materials Needed:

Duct tape in different colors and prints

Scissors

Old hairband

Hot glue

Instructions:

1. Pick a duct tape color of your choice and wrap it around your hairband to completely cover it. Keep it aside.

2. Cut about 6 inches to 8 inches of duct tape strips to create your rosettes.

3. Fold the duct tape lengthwise, leaving a little sticky strip of the duct tape exposed.

4. Use your fingers to do away with the wrinkles and air bubbles and flatten the duct tape fold.

5. Fold one edge of the tape at one end to create a small triangle. Again, you must leave the little sticky strip exposed.

6. Hold the duct tape at the folded triangular end and start rolling the duct tape.

7. Make sure to use the sticky edge to adhere the rosette together as you roll.

8. Hot glue the rosette onto your duct tape covered hairband.

9. Create a few small and large sized rosettes to make a beautiful bunch of roses on your hairband.

1. Cover hair band with duct tape

2. Now put aside the hairband

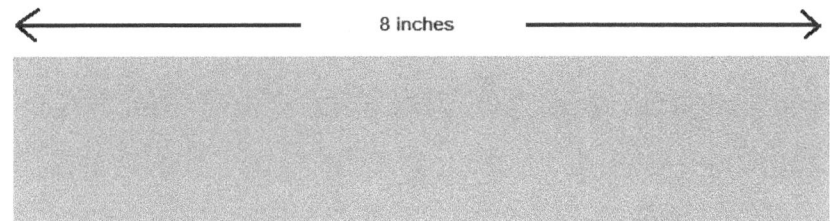

3. Cut about 8 inches of tape for the rosette

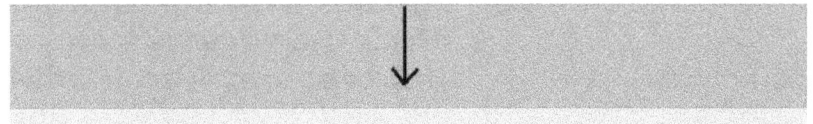

4. Fold it lengthwise, leaving a little sticky edge

5. Fold one edge into a triangle

6. Fold the tip and start rolling the duct tape around it, sticking as you move forward

7. The rosette will take shape, then close the end with a dab of glue. Stick the rosettes on your duct tape covered hairband

Project 32 – Decorative Designer Shoes

Make a fashion statement with duct tape covered shoes. Your old shoes can be covered with printed duct tape to give them a new look and also making them waterproof. This project requires a bit of skill and patience.

Materials Needed:

Duct tape in a print of your choice

Fine tip marker

Exact-O knife

Cutting surface

Old pair of slippers/shoes

Instructions:

1. Work on a cutting surface and start with the sides of your shoes. Cut and connect several pieces of duct tape lengthwise as big enough to capture the side profile of your shoe with a little extra room for tracing. Place this piece down and trace the outline of the side with a fine tip marker.

2. Carefully cut out the pattern with the Exact-O knife.

3. Adhere the cut out to the side of the shoe, use the knife to fine-tune the pattern.

4. Continue the steps on the other side of the shoe as well as the front, making sure to leave holes open for the laces.

5. Use the same design duct tape or use a contrasting color to cover the shoe tongue. You can change the pattern whenever you like and step out in style every time!

Project 33 – Decorative Belt

Whether your belt breaks or you forget to wear it in the morning, the belt-less day is one of the longest of the year. Instead of pulling your pants up every other second, grab a few items lying around and make yourself one of these stylish duct tape belts.

Materials Needed:

Duct tape

Scissors

Punch

Instructions:

1. Take a long piece of tape and wrap it around your body with the sticky side out. This will give you the approximate measurement of the belt.

2. Cut the tape off the roll at the length that fits around your waist. Add several inches to be on the safer side, which can be later tucked into the belt loop.

3. Cut a second piece of tape the same length as the first.

4. Place the two pieces together, sticky side to sticky side and adhere them together to form a long duct tape fabric strip.

5. Take the punch or a pen to make holes on the end of your belt.

6. Cut a second piece of duct tape at a much shorter length and fold it together, then in a circle to make a belt loop. Connect this belt loop with more tape a few inches in from the side without holes.

7. Put yarn through the two belt holes to keep it in place or wrap duct tape around the belt for a one-time use.

This style of duct tape belt will eventually start to stretch and possibly tear, but it will definitely get you through the annoying belt-less day.

1. Measure the length of duct tape needed by passing it around your waist

2. Join 2 pieces of ape together to form a duct tape fabric strip

3. Punch out holes on one end

4. Make a belt loop with a 2nd piece of duct tape

5. Use belt to get you through a belt-less day

Project 34 – Fashionable Clutch Bag

Sometimes all a girl needs is an accessory to complete her look. But many times it is not possible to find a matching piece in your collection. Duct tape can help you craft a shiny new clutch bag of your own with very basic requirements.

You will need:

Craft paper in white

Duct tape in a print or color of your choice

X-ACTO knife

Ruler

Scissors

Velcro squares

Instructions:

1. Make a rectangle on your sheet of paper measuring about 12 inches x 18 inches.

2. Cut the rectangle and this is the base of your clutch bag.

3. Fold the paper such that it is equally divided into thirds measuring about 6 inches each.

4. On the top flap measure the center horizontally. This will also be about 6 inches in the middle.

5. Now cut a triangle from the center going outwards thus creating the flap of your clutch bag.

6. Open up the paper and flip it over. Cover the topside with duct tape creating a pattern of your choice.

7. Once again flip it over so that the duct tape side is at the back.

8. Once again fold the paper into thirds along the crease you had made earlier to create an envelope. You clutch bag will begin to take shape.

9. Seal the sides with duct tape leaving just the flap open.

10. Adhere Velcro on the top flap and the front of the clutch bag and you are good to go!

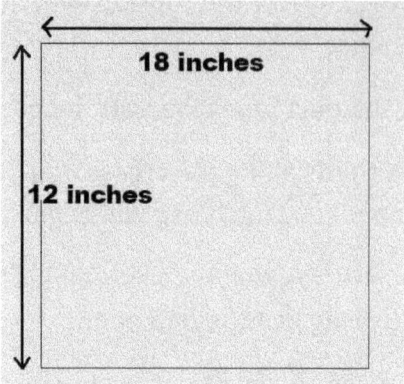

1. Cut a rectangle 12 x 18 inches from a white craft paper sheet

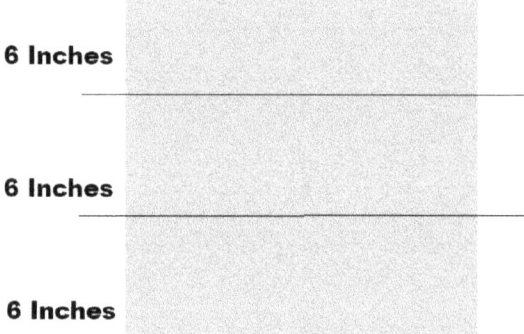

2. Divide the rectangle into thirds, 6 inches each

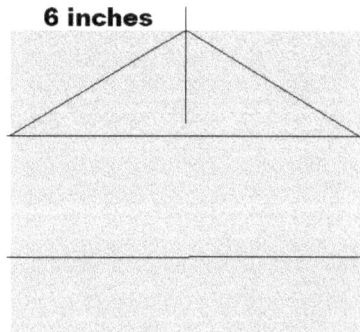

3. Measure the center (6 inches) at the top and cut a triangle to make the flap of the clutch

4. Cover one side of the paper with duct tape

5. Flip over and create an envelope by folding the bottom flap up. Seal the two sides with duct tape

6. Add a velcro on the top of the flap and front of the clutch

Project 35 - Star Earrings

Making your own earrings to match your outfits or gifting them to friends can be fun. It is easy and quick and you hardly need any supplies. As far as the designs are concerned, sky is the limit. With a little bit of creativity, you can make a pair of new earrings everyday with duct tape.

Materials Needed:

Duct tape in various colors and prints

Scissors

Craft paper

Fine tip marker

Hot glue or clamps

Earring hooks

Instructions:

1. Take a piece of duct tape about 12 inches in length and fold it over to make it into a duct tape fabric strip.

2. The fabric strip will now be approximately 6 inches in length. You can vary the length and width depending on the design you want to create.

3. Draw the design you want to shape your earring in on a piece of craft paper with a fine tip marker. In this case, draw a star.

4. Cut the design and this is your basic pattern.

5. Now lay the design on your fabric sheet and trace the outline with the fine tip marker.

6. Cut out the duct tape fabric sheet according to the shape of the star.

7. Now use a clamp or hot glue to adhere the earring hook to one of the points on the star.

8. Repeat to make a pair.

9. You can make different designs using basic patterns. Try using cookie cutters as patterns for large earrings.

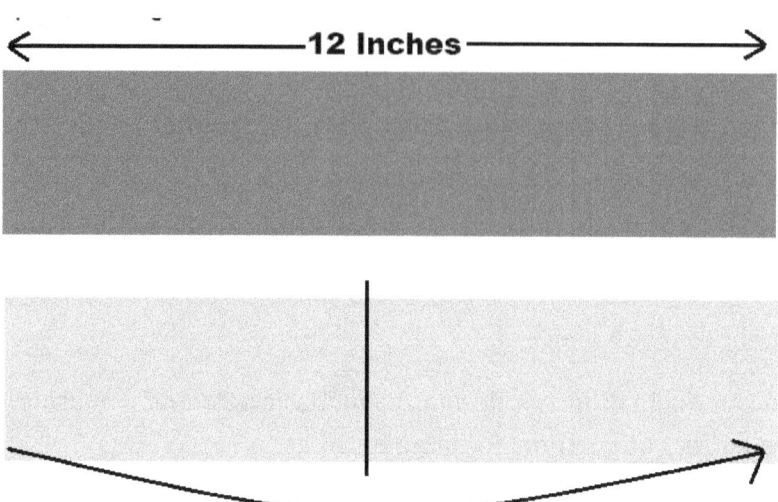

1. Cut a 12 inch strip and fold over

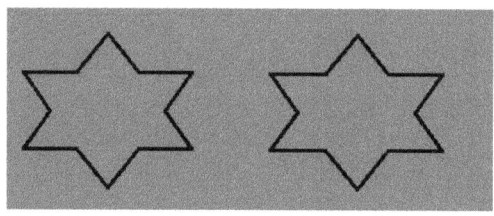

2. Trace the star pattern on the tape and cut

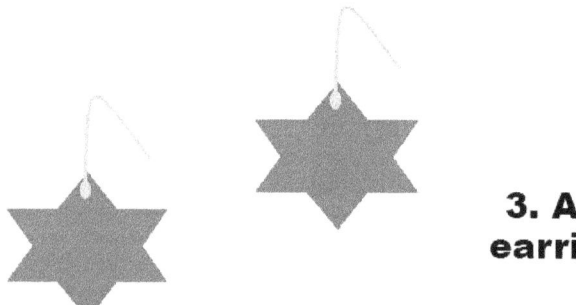

3. Attach the earring hooks

Project 36 – Beaded Necklace

Beads are a popular trend these days. Finding the perfect beaded necklace can be a tough job, but you can create one of your own at home. Choose various colors that you like and mix and match different sizes of beads to create a variation.

Materials Needed:

Duct tape in various colors

Cutting board

X-ACTO knife

Ruler

Toothpick

Piece of string

Instructions:

1. Cut a few strips of duct tape in a color or print of your choice.

2. Lay the strips on a cutting board and cut them into half lengthwise.

3. You can further cut them to make smaller beads. It is good to experiment with a few sizes to find your perfect bead.

4. Next, find the center of your strip and cut it diagonally across such that the cutting line meets the top corner. The resulting strip will look like a thin and long triangle.

5. Take a thin object like a toothpick and wet it with water.

6. Take the broadest end of the duct tape strip and wet that with water as well. This is so that the duct tape does not stick onto the toothpick.

7. Roll the duct tape strip tightly onto the toothpick moving from the broader end to the thinner end.

8. Slip the bead off the toothpick and you are ready to make your bead necklace. Create several such beads with different colors and sizes.

9. String different colors of beads together to form the necklace.

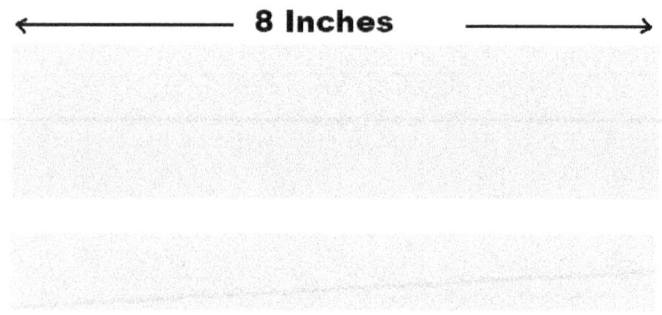

1. Cut an 8 inch strip into halves

2. Cut another 8 inch strip diagonally across the middle

3. Start with the broad end of the duct tape and wrap on the tooth pick

4. Slip the bead off the tooth pick and string together to from a necklace

Party & Holiday Projects

Project 37 – Party Mask

If you are hosting a theme party for the kids, why not give them a chance to style their own party masks out of duct tape? Party masks are easy to make and with a little help the kids will be able to make their own.

Materials Needed:

Duct tape in various prints depending on the theme of your party

Scissors

Craft paper

Fine tip marker

Elastic band

Punch

X-ACTO knife

Instructions:

1. Draw the shape of the mask you want to create on craft paper.

2. Cut out holes for the eyes and keep it aside. This is your basic pattern. You can make different shapes of the mask.

3. Make a duct tape fabric sheet by following instructions from the basic duct tape fabric guide.

4. Trace the pattern of the mask on the duct tape sheet.

5. Cut the duct tape fabric sheet along the tracing.

6. Cut out the eye sockets using an X-ACTO knife.

7. Punch a hole on the two ends of the mask and tie an elastic band through both the holes to wear it around the face.

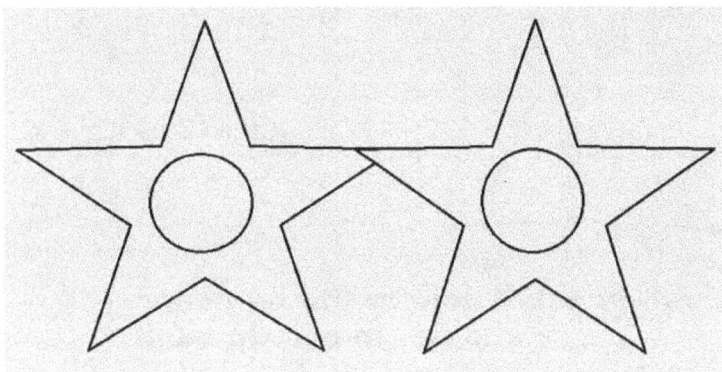

1. Draw a shape of your mask on craft paper and cut out pattern

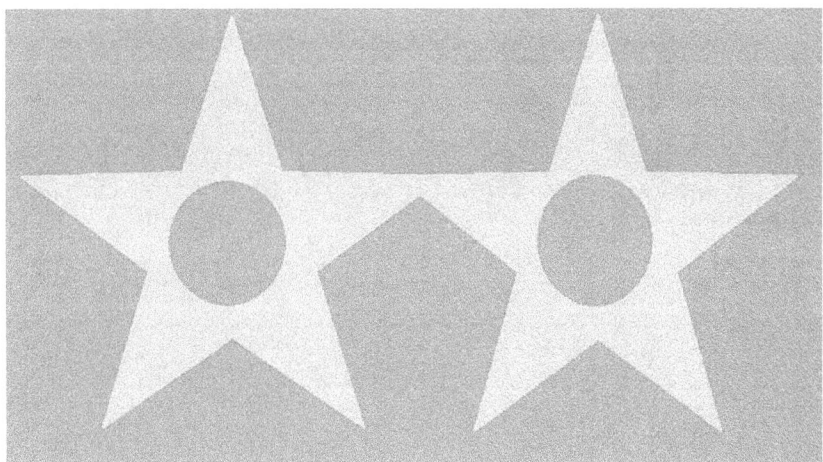

2. Trace pattern on a duct tabe fabric sheet in your color of choice

3. Cut out the duct tape as per the tracing lines and cut out the eye sockets

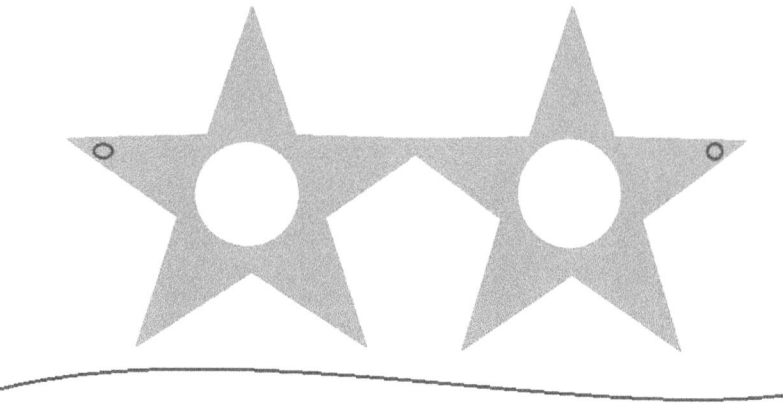

4. Punch a hole at the two ends and tie an elastic band

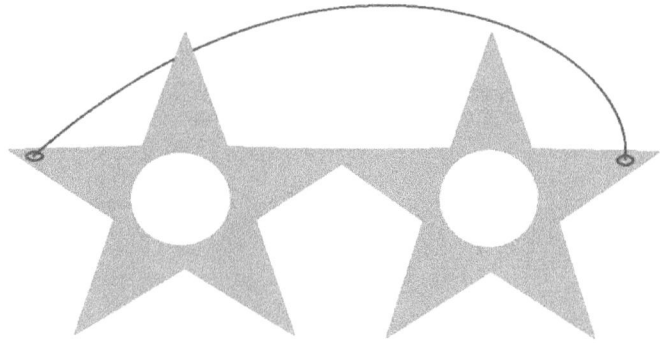

5. Enjoy the party!

Project 38 – Holiday Ornament

With minimal supplies, you can craft a duct tape holiday ornament that will last you and your family many years of tradition. This is easy enough to keep the kids busy for a while.

Materials Needed:

Foam ball

Duct tape

Pipe cleaner

Scissors

Instructions:

1. Cover the foam ball completely in duct tape, using small pieces to make sure that the white of the ball is well covered.

2. This ornament will have a thick, wrinkly texture. In order to accomplish this cut small strips of duct tape and crinkle it down the middle, leaving a little sticky adhesive at the bottoms and tops for attaching to the ball.

3. Continue putting the crinkles strips of duct tape around the covered foam ball until it is covered

4. Cut the pipe cleaner down at an adequate length to make a hook. Loop the pipe cleaner and attach it to the ornament with duct tape.

5. Hang it on your Christmas tree! You can further decorate it with small family photos or encouraging words.

1. Cover the foam ball with duct tape

2. Cut thin strips of tape and crinkle them leaving a little adhesive

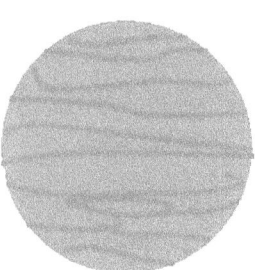

3. Cover the ball with crinkled duct tape layers

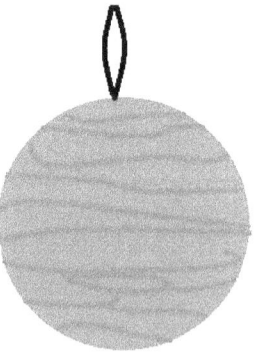

4. Attach a pipecleaner as a hook and hang on your tree or mantle

Project 39 – Holiday Wreath

A wreath is a holiday staple as far as home decorations go. Why limit yourself to adorning your home with only the design that is available in the stores? Instead, create your own holiday wreath out of duct tape or as a gift for others.

Materials Needed:

Styrofoam wreath form

Green duct tape

Red duct tape

Scissors

Instructions:

1. Cut about 5 inches of green duct tape.

2. Fold the top corners down and in to make a little triangle, but leave a little sticky adhesive bit left at the bottom.

3. Attach the first piece of tape on the wreath from directly in the center.

4. Continue the process of folding and attach each piece to form rows of pointed duct tape. The duct tape should be adhered such that it completely covers the foam base with pointy tops.

5. Take a large strip of red duct tape to make a bow and attach it to the bottom of the wreath.

6. You can decorate the wreath with duct tape flowers little bows etc. Hang it at your front door to welcome guests in style.

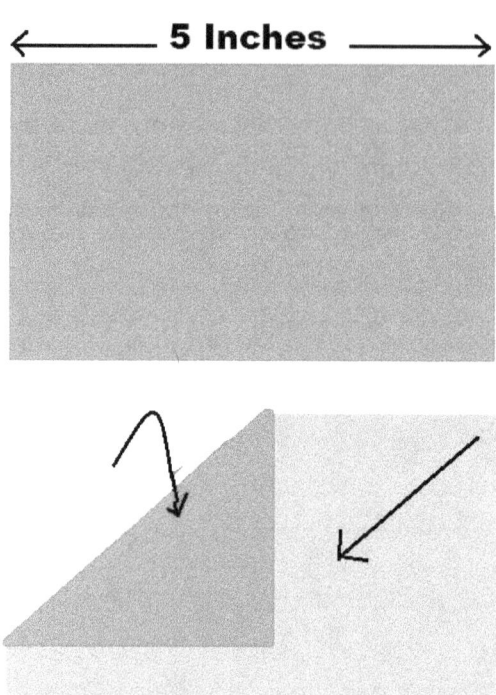

1. Fold the top left and right down to form a triangle, leaving a little adhesive at the bottom

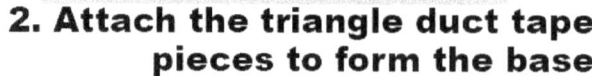

2. Attach the triangle duct tape pieces to form the base

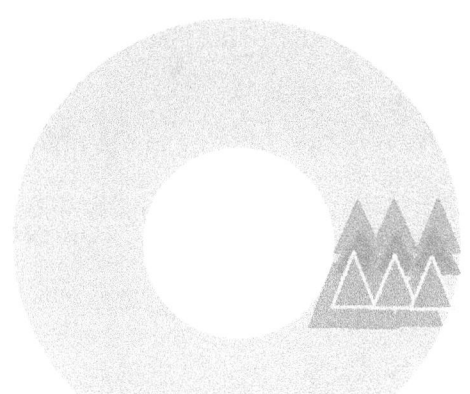

3. Overlap the entire wreath with green triangles

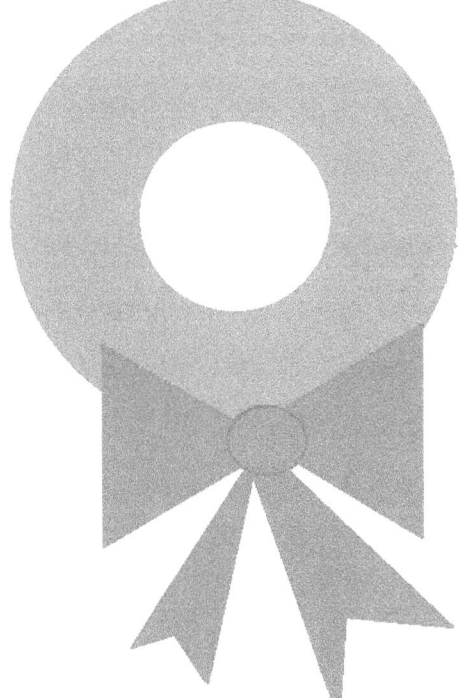

4. Decorate your wreath with a large duct tape ribbon

Project 40 - Candy Cane

Duct tape candy canes are a great option to bring in the holiday cheer without the extra pounds.

Materials Needed:

An old pen

Jewelry wire

Red duct tape

White duct tape

Scissors

Instructions:

1. Wrap the jewelry wire around the nib side of the old pen, forming the candy cane hook. Be careful when twisting the wire.

2. Cover the pen and curved part completely in red duct tape.

3. Wrap the curved part of the candy cane a few more times so that it comes close to the same thickness as the body part of the pen.

4. Cut a piece of the white duct tape into thirds out of a relatively long strip.

5. Wrap the white duct tape pieces at an angle around the red duct tape to give the candy cane look.

6. Make a little loop with white duct tape and hang your candy cane.

Project 41 – Gift bags

Let's make unique gift bags out of old cereal boxes and contribute towards eco-friendly living. Your friends will love these! These are great for packing party favors or hostess gifts.

Materials Needed:

Empty cereal boxes

Duct tape in various colors

Scissors

Ribbon

Punch

X-ACTO knife

Instructions:

1. Cut off the top flaps of your cereal box with the X-ACTO knife.

2. Choose 3 to 4 different patterns and colors of duct tape to make your gift bag interesting.

3. You can alternate the different designs or create a pattern of your choice. It is a good idea to roughly sketch the layout of the different patterns.

4. Start from the bottom with duct tape pattern number one and run it along all four sides of the cereal box.

5. Make sure you press the tape down as you go to avoid air bubbles and wrinkles.

6. Follow the layout you created until the entire box is covered with duct tape. Overlap every strip of tape by about ½ inch as you go to the top.

7. Smoothen the top of the cereal box by folding over 1 inch of duct tape inside the box.

8. Punch out two holes in the center of the cereal box on either side.

9. Cut your ribbon into two pieces of about 10 inches each.

10. String the ribbon through each hole to make the handles. Tie a knot to secure all the sides.

11. Decorate your gift bag with duct tape flowers, bows and other decorations.

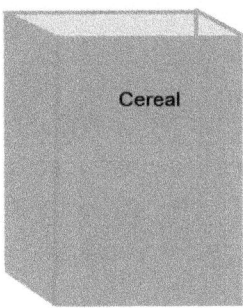

1. Cut the top flaps of an empty cereal box

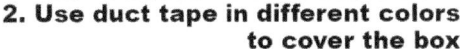

2. Use duct tape in different colors to cover the box

3. Cover the box with duct tape and punch two holes for handles on each side

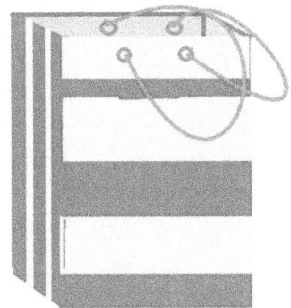

Project 42 – Tassel Garlands

Tassel garlands can add a cheerful appeal to your party, but making one out of tissue paper can be expensive. Here is a great idea to make a tassel garland out of duct tape. You can also attach tassel garlands to balloons and make them even more beautiful.

Materials Needed:

Duct tape in various colors

Scissors

Ruler

Twine

Hot glue

Instructions:

1. Make a duct tape sheet. Your sheet should be approximately 12 inches long and 5 inches wide. You can increase or decrease the dimensions if you like.

2. Fold your duct tape sheet at about one inch from the top and make a crease.

3. Now start cutting fringes from the bottom and stop at the crease marking. This step needs to be carefully monitored or you may end up cutting the fringe off

4. Keep a distance of approximately 1/4th inch between each fringe. Remember that closer the distance between two fringes, the more fluffily your tassel.

5. Once the entire sheet is cut into fringes, start rolling it tightly from one end.

6. Dab a dot of hot glue and secure the end for your tassel to take shape.

7. To make a loop, cut a piece twine and secure it on the top of the tassel with a piece of duct tape.

8. Make about 12 to 15 tassels and string them together with the twine to make your tassel garland.

Project 43 – Gift Wrap Bows

An easy alternative to a gift-wrapping ribbon bow is a duct tape bow. It is much sturdier and cost efficient. Duct tape bows can be made in advance and used later when required.

Materials Needed:

Duct tape in various colors

Scissors

X-ACTO knife

Instructions:

1. Pull out about 18 inches of red duct tape (or any other color you like).

2. Leave about 1 inch of adhesive at one end and fold the tape over.

3. Adhere the two sticky sides of tape pressing with your fingers. Remove any air bubbles or wrinkles that may form.

4. Next, take the two edges and stick them together to form a circular cuff.

5. Slightly flatten the circular cuff and pinch the tape together at the center so it starts to look like a bow.

6. Take about 3 inches of duct tape from the roll and cut a strip of about 1/4th inch.

7. Wrap the strip of tape around the center of the bow to hold it together.

8. Cut two more strips of about 10 inches each. Fold them over like you did in steps 2 and 3.

9. Adhere the tails to the back of the bow at an angle.

10. Snip a little bit of the bottom at a slant.

11. Go ahead and dress up your gift with your duct tape bow.

Project 44 - Christmas Stockings

While sewing up a stocking is an advanced project, simple duct tape can be used to add a stylish and sentimental touch to your mantel. Use duct tape to create a stocking this Christmas!

Materials Needed:

Duct tape in various colors and patterns

Scissors

Old newspaper

Pencil

Instructions:

1. Cut out two stocking patterns out of the newspaper. You can lay an old stocking and trace out the pattern if you have one available.

2. Cover both the pieces of newspaper on one side with the duct tape pattern of your choice.

3. Keep the newspaper side on the inside, and attach the two stocking patterns by edging them with a separate piece of duct tape.

4. Add a contrasting color to the top and heel of the stocking to give it an authentic look.

5. Write a name on the top of the stocking with either duct tape or the traditional glue and glitter and you've got a durable homemade stocking to show off!

1. Cut 2 pieces of stocking pattern from a newspaper

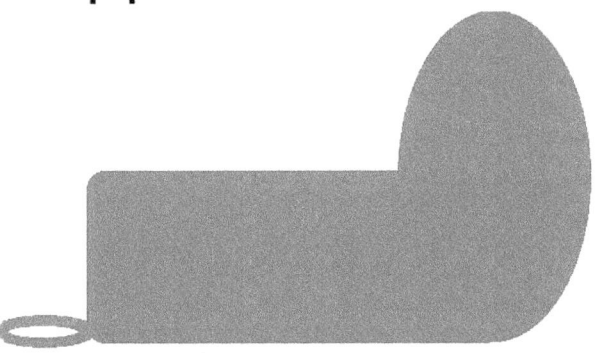

2. Cover both pieces with duct tape and conjoin them with more tape

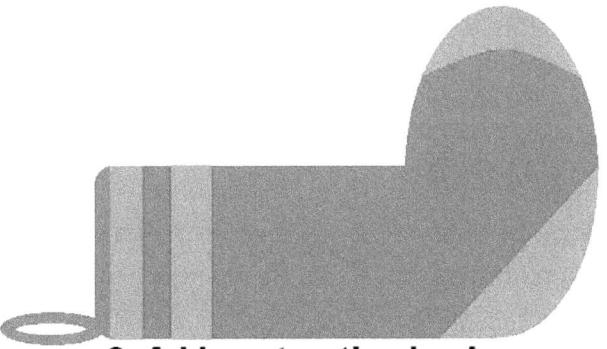

3. Add contrasting heel and top for decoration

Project 45 - Inexpensive Holiday Wrapping Paper

Create your own Santa gift-wrapping using only duct tape. It will be a tough exercise for the recipients to open up, but worth the wait!

Materials Needed:

Red duct tape

Black duct tape

Gold duct tape

Scissors

Newspaper

Instructions:

1. Wrap your gift box with the newspaper. This project works great on boxes that are fairly large in size. You can experiment with different duct tape colors to create a style of your own.

2. Cover up the newspaper covered box completely with red duct tape. This is the base of Santa's suit

3. Wrap one or two black bands of duct tape around the middle of the box to represent Santa's belt.

4. Create the belt buckle by taking four strips of gold duct tape and fashioning them into a rectangle in the middle of the black band.

5. Your gifts will stand out under the Christmas tree!

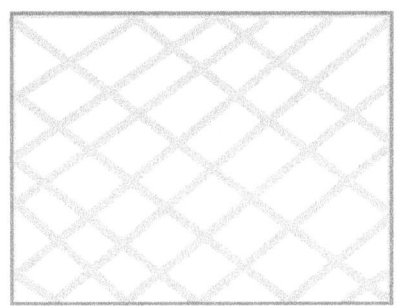
1. Cover your gift box with newspaper

2. Wrap it with red duct tape

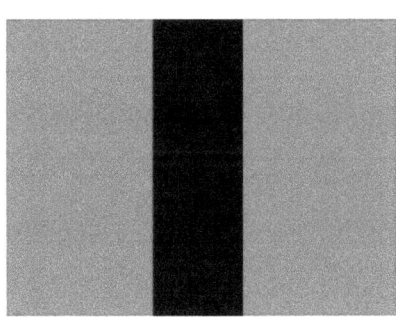
3. Wrap a band of black duct tape to make a belt

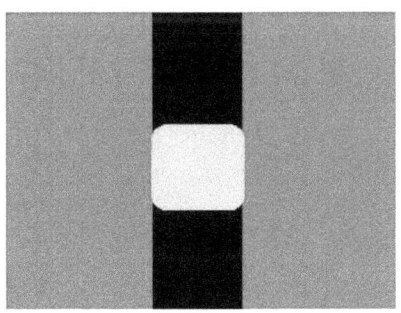
4. Add piece of gold tape to complete the gift wrap

Project 46 – Decorative Glass Bottles

There is a growing trend of using glass bottles and jars both in the pantry and for parties. You can use duct tape to add a fun element to plain old glass bottles and canning jars. Different duct tape patterns can also be used to distinguish glass canisters in the kitchen as well.

Materials Needed:

Duct tape in various colors and patterns

Glass bottles and jars

Scissors

Measuring tape

Instructions:

1. Measure around the circumference of your glass bottles and jars.

2. Choose exciting prints and patterns to perk up these glass bottles and jars.

3. Cut a length of duct tape according to the measurement.

4. Further cut the duct tape into thinner strips.

5. Adhere the strips around the glass bottles and jars to create interesting patterns.

6. Add matching paper straws to the glass bottle.

7. You can use a fine tip market to write names on the duct tape.

Project 47 – Gift Tags

No gift is complete without a wonderful gift tag. Instead of buying gift tags from the store, make a few easily in the comfort of your home.

Materials Needed:

Cookie cutters in various shapes

Duct tape

Fine tip marker

Scissors

Punch

Baker's twine or ribbon

Instructions:

1. Make a basic duct tape fabric sheet by following instructions from the basic duct tape fabric sheet guide in the beginning of the book.

2. Use large sized cookie cutter to trace interesting shapes on your duct tape fabric sheet using a fine tip marker.

3. Use cookie cutters depending on the occasion (Christmas tree for the holidays, a pumpkin for thanksgiving and balloons for birthdays).

4. Cut the shapes according to the traced lines.

5. Punch a hole at the top and string the baker's twine or a piece of ribbon through it.

6. Use a fine tip marker to write your wishes on the gift tag and attach it to the gift.

Project 48 – Cupcake Flags

A cupcake that is decorated with little cupcake flags is twice the fun. You can use individual flags to decorate cupcakes or stacks of pancakes. This is a great way to get the party started. The flags can be used as placeholders and nametags as well when laying a dinner table for guests. Insert these flags into fruits and decorate the table with style.

Materials Needed:

Duct tape in various prints and patterns

Scissors

Toothpicks or bamboo skewers for taller flags

Instructions:

1. Cut a piece of duct tape and snip it into half from the middle depending on the size of the flag you need.

2. Lay the piece of tape horizontally lengthwise with the sticky side facing up.

3. Find the center and place a toothpick or bamboo skewer vertically.

4. Fold the left sticky side onto the right sticky side sandwiching the toothpick in the middle.

5. Cut a small triangle from the edge to create a flag.

6. Decorate your flag with names and push them into the cupcakes.

1. Cut duct tape piece in half

2. Place toothpick in the middle and fold over

3. Cut triangle at the edge and decorate

www.ingramcontent.com/pod-product-compliance
Lightning Source LLC
Chambersburg PA
CBHW051811170526
45167CB00005B/1962